A Litter
Bit of Humor

Laughs, sayings & reminders
to think paws-itive!

Inspired by Faith

A Litter Bit of Humor
ISBN 978-0-9853005-9-3

Published by Product Concept Mfg., Inc.
2175 N. Academy Circle #200, Colorado Springs, CO 80909

Written and Compiled by Patricia Mitchell
in association with Product Concept Mfg., Inc.

All scripture quotations are from the King James version
of the Bible unless otherwise noted.

Scriptures taken from the Holy Bible,
New International Version®, NIV®.
Copyright © 1973, 1978, 1984 by Biblica, Inc.™
Used by permission of Zondervan.
All rights reserved worldwide.
www.zondervan.com

Sayings not having a credit listed are contributed by writers
for Product Concept Mfg., Inc. or in a rare case,
the author is unknown.

A Litter
Bit of Humor

Never feed your cat anything
    that doesn't match the carpet.

Could you use a smile today? Or how about a wise word to encourage, or simple truism to inspire? Maybe even a little reminder that no matter what else is going on, there's always something to feel good about.

A Litter Bit of Humor is a book of witty remarks, timeless truths, and classic quotations, along with a smattering of jokes and groaners. Sprinkled throughout are funny, laugh-with-me photos designed to tickle the cat lover's—and everybody else's—heart. After all, we all appreciate a paws-itive thought, and any day is a good day for a lighthearted look at the world.

Open to any page, and you'll find a purrfect reason to smile!

Ambition is a great thing, but it sure can get you into a lot of hard work.

**Be careful about reading health books.
You may die of a misprint.**
Mark Twain

Keep cool:
it will be all one a hundred years hence.
Ralph Waldo Emerson

**Sometimes the littlest things
in life are the hardest to take.
You can sit on a mountain more
comfortable than on a tack.**

Proverbial Wisecracks

- Laugh and the world laughs with you; cry and you have to blow your nose.

- If you can't stand the heat, install air conditioning.

- Better be safe than try to give a cat a bath.

- The pen is mightier than the sword, but it had better be a really big pen.

"I'm afraid that hairball has to come out."

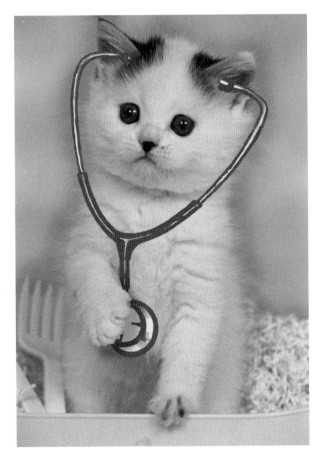

There are people who,
instead of listening to what is being said
to them, are already listening to what
they are going to say themselves.
Albert Guinon

**The oldest, shortest words—
"yes" and "no"—are those which
require the most thought.**
Pythagoras

Then is then. Now is now.
We must grow to learn the difference.

**There is no cosmetic
for beauty like happiness.**
Marguerite Blessington

How the Cat Sees Things

If things can go wrong,
it's wrong they will go,
And you don't need nine lives
to know this is so.

There's no sense in fuming,
and no sense in fretting—
Just figure that better and better
it's gotta be getting!

De Best

A teacher challenged her students to write a sentence using the words Defeat, Defense, Deduct, and Detail. After a few minutes, one student put down his pencil and raised his hand. Surprised he finished so quickly, the teacher asked the student to read his sentence aloud.

With a smile of satisfaction, he said, "Defeat of deduct went over defense before detail."

When things go wrong,
it's kinda fun to act like
everything's just fine and see if
anyone bothers to fill you in.

**This time, like all times,
is a very good one, if we but
know what to do with it.**
Ralph Waldo Emerson

A farmer with too many chickens
posted this sign on the coop:
"Free chickens.
Our coop runneth over."

Mother Tongue

A mother mouse and a baby mouse were walking along, and suddenly a cat pounced right in front of them. The mother mouse yelled, "Woof, woof," and the cat turned tail and scampered away.

"Now you see," said the mother mouse to her baby, "why I insist that you learn a foreign language!"

Wake me when all the dogs
have been sent to the moon.

Grace

A longtime church member died and appeared at the Pearly Gates. Peter told him that he needed 100 points to get into heaven. Peter said, "Tell me all the good things you have done, and I'll keep score."

"Sure," the man replied. "I've gone to church every single Sunday of my life."

"Good," Peter said. "One point."

"And I've served on every committee there is, taught Sunday school, and visited shut-ins."

"Wonderful! One point."

The man was beginning to get nervous. "For the last 20 years," he ventured, "I spent every Thanksgiving and Christmas downtown at the soup kitchen to feed the homeless."

"One point," said Peter.

Exasperated, the man cried, "At this rate, I'll get into heaven only by the grace of God!"

"That's right!" exclaimed Peter as he swung open the gates. "Come on in!"

Show me...

...a cat that ate a lemon,
   and I'll show you a sour puss.

...an optimist,
   and I'll show you a happy-condriac.

...a skimpy dress,
   and I'll show you a cold shoulder.

...a waffle iron,
   and I'll show you a place to take your
   wrinkled waffles.

...a singing cricket,
   and I'll show you a humbug.

...a stolen sausage,
   and I'll show you a missing link.

Woman: My doctor told me to drink carrot juice after a hot bath.

Friend: Did you like the juice?

Woman: I haven't gotten to it yet. I'm still drinking the hot bath.

A keychain is a handy device that allows you to lose all your keys at once rather than one key once in a while.

**Anybody can give advice—
the trouble comes in finding someone
interested in taking it.**

There's nothing more annoying than arguing with somebody who actually knows what he's talking about.

You can tell by your toes whether or not it's raining. If they're wet, it's raining.

To err is human, but to really mess things up you need a computer.

Q&A Time

Q: Is it unlucky to have a black cat cross your path?
A: Only if you're a mouse.

Q: Why did the mama cat put stamps on her kittens?
A: She wanted to mail a litter.

Q: What's the difference between a cat and a comma?
A: A cat has its claws at the end of its paws, while a comma is a pause at the end of a clause.

Q: How do we know that Adam and Eve were noisy?
A: They raised Cain!

Q: Which way did the IT guy go?
A: He went data way!

Q: Who is the most successful financier in the Bible?
A: Noah. He was floating his stock while everyone else was in liquidation.

Q: Why is it hard for a submarine captain to live on his salary?
A: Because he can't keep his head above water.

It was so hot that summer
that the farmer fed his chickens
cracked ice so they wouldn't
lay hard-boiled eggs.

**Why do kids get a
growth spurt a week after you've
bought them new clothes?**

The neighbor's old dog is so lazy
that he only chases parked cars.

**Laughter is the sun that drives
winter from the human face.**
Victor Hugo

Job Descriptions in Plain English

What they say...

What they mean.

Must be detail-oriented.

There are no proofreaders, fact checkers, or quality control.

Must be able to work at a fast pace.

We have no time to train you, and we're already six months behind.

Problem-solving skills required.

We've got problems.

Leadership skills required.

You're expected to do management-level work without the title or salary to go with it.

Hope works in these ways: it looks for the good in people instead of harping on the worst; it discovers what can be done instead of grumbling about what cannot; it regards problems, large or small, as opportunities; it pushes ahead when it would be easy to quit; it "lights the candle" instead of cursing the darkness.

**Some call it an aquarium.
I call it lunch.**

Rest Stop

A woman opened her front door one afternoon and found a cat sitting on her porch. She stooped down to pet the animal, and immediately he scampered inside, jumped in an armchair, curled up, and went to sleep. Several hours later, the cat awoke, meowed at the door, and the woman let him out. This went on for several days.

Curious as to where the cat lived, the woman attached a note to his collar that read, "I'd like to know who owns this nice, gentle cat. He's been spending every afternoon at my house curled up on a chair taking a nap."

The next day, the cat returned to the woman's house with a new note attached to his collar. She opened the note and read the following: "He lives in a home with three children under six and a newborn, and he's trying to catch up on his sleep. If you have another chair, do you mind if I come with him tomorrow?"

Golf Lesson

A young man who loved to golf found himself with a few free hours one afternoon. He figured if he got to the golf course and played quickly, he could get in nine holes before heading back to the office.

Just as he was about to tee off, an older gentleman approached and asked to join him. The young man had no choice but to agree. Though the old gent couldn't hit the ball far, he played fairly quickly and didn't waste time on the course.

When the two reached the ninth fairway, the young man was confronted with a tough shot: a large pine tree sat right between his ball and the hole.

"You know," the old man said, "when I was your age, I'd hit the ball right over that tree."

Challenged, the younger golfer considered his strategy, swung hard, and gave the ball a sharp, well-aimed send-off. The ball soared, but then smacked into the tree trunk and landed barely a foot from where it had started out.

"Of course," the old man continued, "when I was your age, that pine tree was only three feet tall."

Enjoy yourself.
These are the "good old days"
you're going to miss in the future.

**Whoever said money can't
buy happiness simply
didn't know where to shop.**

Always acknowledge a fault.
This will throw those in authority
off their guard and give you an
opportunity to commit more.
Mark Twain

**After all is said and done,
a lot more will have been said
than done.**

Some cause happiness
wherever they go;
others, whenever they go.
Oscar Wilde

**Remember, work like a dog;
nap like a cat; eat like a horse;
think like a fox; and visit your
veterinarian every year.**

A genius is someone who
shoots at something no one else
can see—and hits it.

**You can discover more about
a person in an hour of play than
in a year of conversation.**
Plato

It's going to be a bad day when...

- You put both contact lenses in the same eye.

- Your silk flowers wither.

- You get a paper cut from a get-well card.

- You come out of your memory-improvement class and forget where you parked your car.

- You bend over to pick a four-leaf clover and you grab a fist full of poison ivy.

- You turn on the news and they're displaying emergency routes out of the city.

- Your teenager comes in from the garage and asks what's covered under your car insurance.

Call a dog,
and he'll come to you.
Call a cat, and she'll take a message
(maybe).

**To make your dreams come true,
you have to stay awake.**

In every family tree,
you can find a few nuts.

**My computer crashed,
and now I have no idea
who my friends are!**

Good Thought

Before you take up cross-country skiing,
move to a small country.

It may be true that it's a small world,
but don't volunteer to paint it.

Don't test the depth of a river with
both feet.

Never eat a sticky bun while brushing
a long-haired cat.

Never hire an electrician with no
eyebrows.

Always take time for a pet-icure.

Ooops!

The bride asks, "Dear, do you have a good memory for faces?"

"I sure do!" hubby replies confidently. "Why do you ask?"

She says, "Because I just broke your shaving mirror."

Heard about that really
exclusive hotel that opened downtown?
Even room service has
an unlisted number.

A friend is always happy
about your successes—as long as they
don't surpass his own.

Never boast about how much you
know. After all, even a leaf of lettuce
knows more than you do. It knows if the
light in the refrigerator really goes out
after the door is shut.

Heard about the optometrists
who came to town and acted up?
They really made spectacles
of themselves.

**Believe it:
There's no snooze button
on a cat who wants breakfast.**

In times of difficulty,
friendship is on trial.
Proverb

**Rain is something that
makes flowers grow
and taxis disappear.**

How come...

- Cat hairs stick to everything except the cat?

- Abbreviated is an eleven-letter word?

- Greyhounds aren't grey?

- Glue doesn't stick to the inside of the bottle?

- Sponges in the ocean haven't soaked up all the water yet?

- Someone doesn't make mouse-flavored cat food?

- Wise guys and wise men are completely different kinds of people?

- A round pizza comes in a square box?

- The driver behind you is always the first to see the light turn green?

- Woolly sheep don't shrink in the rain?

History repeats itself,
especially if you fail the course.

**Worry is the interest paid
on trouble before it falls due.**
W. R. Inge

It is impossible to enjoy
idling thoroughly, unless one
has plenty of work to do.
Jerome K. Jerome

**The only food that doesn't go up
in price is food for thought.**

The person willing to roll
up his sleeves rarely loses his shirt.

**There is just one life
for each of us: our own.**
Euripides

Those who do not pray when
the sun is shining will not know how
when the storm clouds gather.

Animals are such agreeable friends—
they ask no questions,
they pass no criticisms.
George Eliot

**Gardening is a matter of
your enthusiasm holding up until
your back gets used to it.**

Life is a shipwreck, but we must not
forget to sing in the lifeboats.
Voltaire

**It is not fair to ask of others what you
are not willing to do yourself.**
Eleanor Roosevelt

We should give as we would
receive, cheerfully, quickly, and without
hesitation; for there is no grace in
a benefit that sticks to the fingers.
Seneca

**Gossip is saying behind
their back what you would not
say to their face. Flattery is saying
to their face what you would not
say behind their back.**

I make the most of all that comes
and the least of all that goes.
Sara Teasdale

Moo

The city girl was visiting her cousin, who lived on a farm. As they were walking in the pasture, the city girl exclaimed, "Look at that flock of cows!"

"Herd of cows," her cousin corrected.

"Of course I've heard of cows!" the city girl replied testily. "There's a whole flock of them!"

Everyone must row
with the oars he possesses.
Proverb

**Painting is poetry that is seen rather
than felt, and poetry is painting that is
felt rather than seen.**
Leonardo da Vinci

Only your real friends
will tell you when your face is dirty.
Proverb

Heard about...

- The teenager who thought her parents were too nosy? At least that's what they kept seeing in her diary.

- The tiny cabins on cruise ships? If you drop a hankie, you've got wall-to-wall carpet.

- The man who retired five years ago? His biggest challenge is keeping the boss from finding out.

Diet Plan

Two women were having coffee together when one confided that there were problems in her marriage. "I've been so upset that I've lost ten pounds," she said.

Her friend shook her head sympathetically, and then asked, "Are you seeing a marriage counselor?"

"Oh, no, not yet," her friend replied. "I still have another five pounds to go!"

Remember when...

- A CD was a place to put your money?

- A web was something you swept from the corner of a room?

- A hard drive was a long commute to work?

- A virus was something you had, not your household electronics?

"For your safety,
I have to confiscate your fishsticks."

It's great to be a guy because...

- You can get everything you need for a two-week vacation in one carry-on.

- Your bathroom lines are non-existent.

- Auto mechanics tell you the truth, and repairmen give you an honest quote.

- Gray hair and wrinkles make you look more distinguished.

- Three pairs of shoes are more than enough.

It's great to be a gal because...

- Chocolate can solve 90% of your problems.

- If you don't like sports, you don't have to pretend that you do.

- You can cry when you feel like it.

- We always have food in the fridge, and we know how to cook it.

- We can dress ourselves in the morning, because we know what matches and what doesn't.

Apologize—that way,
you'll always have the last word.

**It is much safer to obey
rather than to rule.**
Thomas à Kempis

If you feel dog tired at night,
it might be because you've been
growling all day long.

**It even helps stupid people
to try hard.**
Seneca

Drag your thoughts away
from your troubles…by the ears,
by the heels, or any other way
you can manage it.
Mark Twain

**People who say that things improve
with age obviously haven't been to their
20th class reunion yet.**

The colder the X-ray table,
the more of your body you
are told to put on it.

Say What?

A man walks into a pet shop. "Got any kittens going cheap?" he asks.

"No, sorry," replies the clerk. "All the ones here just go Meow."

Things you don't want to hear during surgery...

- Hey...what's this?

- Huh...this is something for the textbooks.

- You mean he's not here for hip surgery?

- Whoa...I can see this costing a bundle.

- Oopsie-daisy!

It's a Feline World

Keyboards are for sleeping,
Stairways right for naps...
Your cell phone is for adding
Funny kitten apps.

TP in the bathroom
Is for feline kicks...
All food on kitchen counters
Gets a few good licks.

Curtains hang for climbing,
Carpets spread to shred
And any chair you sit on,
Off! It's now my bed.

Yes, each and every morning,
You can clearly see
The grand old sun arising
Just to shine on me!

Do not be too timid and squeamish about your actions. All life is an experiment. The more experiments you make the better. What if they are a little coarse, and you may get your coat soiled or torn? What if you do fail, and get fairly rolled in the dirt once or twice? Up again, you shall never be so afraid of a tumble.

Ralph Waldo Emerson

A single arrow is easily broken,
but not ten in a bundle.
Proverb

Unity, not uniformity, must be our aim.
We attain unity only through variety.
Differences must be integrated,
not annihilated, not absorbed.
Mary Parker Follett

What one has, one ought to use;
and whatever he does,
he should do with all his might.
Cicero

You know you're getting older when...

- Your most frequently called numbers are those of doctors' offices.

- It gets harder to make ends meet— like the ends of your fingers and toes.

- You begin to question the benefit of gravity.

- You start meeting the kids you used to babysit with kids of their own.

- You realize that a dull evening at home is really nice once in a while.

- You discover that the only programs worth watching are on the nostalgia channel.

- Kids ask you how you could take your phone with you if it was attached to the wall.

- You feel you've finally figured out some answers, but no one's asking you questions.

- You argue passionately about investments and medical insurance plans.

- You actually observe the speed limit and use your turn signals.

- You wonder about kids these days.

"If one more person tells me
to Hang In There,
I'm gonna...
I'm gonna..."

When you have only two pennies left in
the world, buy a loaf of bread with one
and a lily with the other.

Proverb

**If you don't get everything you want,
think of the things you don't get that
you don't want.**

Oscar Wilde

I speak the truth, not so much as I
would, but as much as I dare; and I dare
a little more as I grow older.

Michel de Montaigne

Neighborhood News

Neighbors wondered about a woman who was going door-to-door carrying a paint brush, tubes of paints, and an easel.

"What do you think she's doing?" they asked the one woman on the block who always seemed to know what was going on.

"Oh," replied the woman, "she's canvassing."

Q&A Time

Q: Where does a cat go if he loses his tail?
A: To a retail store, of course!

Q: Where will you find a collection of antique cat toys?
A: In a mewseum.

Q: How do you measure cat food?
A: So much purr cup.

Q: What do you call an overweight cat?
A: A flabby tabby.

I have been through some
terrible things in my life,
some of which actually happened.
Mark Twain

**The best thing one can do
when it's raining is to let it rain.**
Henry Wadsworth Longfellow

Do not protect yourself by a fence,
but rather by your friends.
Proverb

Street Smarts

As a pedestrian crossed the street, a car suddenly appeared, aiming right at him. The man started to run, but the car sped up. Hoping to dash back to the curb, he turned around, only to see the car change lanes. Terrified, he froze as the car whizzed past him, missing him by an inch. The car screeched to a halt, and the driver's window came down. A squirrel popped his head out. "See?" he yelled at the man, "now you know how it feels!"

There are no foreign lands.
It is the traveler only who is foreign.
Robert Louis Stevenson

**Always laugh when you can.
It is cheap medicine.
Lord Byron**

The secret to being miserable
is to have leisure to bother about
whether you are happy or not.
George Bernard Shaw

Mouse Musings

One afternoon three mice were sitting around boasting about their strength. The first mouse said, "Mousetraps are jokes! I do push-ups with the bar!"

The second mouse stood up, pulled a pill from his pocket, and swallowed it. "That, pal," the mouse announced with a grin, "was rat poison!"

The third mouse yawned and got up to leave. "Hey!" said the first mouse, "where do you think you're going?"

"It's time for me to go home and chase the cat."

I have not failed.
I've just found 10,000 ways
that won't work.
Thomas Alva Edison

**Everyone excels in something
in which another fails.**
Proverb

Money doesn't grow on trees;
you've got to beat the bushes for it.

Flattery is like cologne—
good to be sniffed,
but not swallowed.

Good Question!

What would you look like playing the piano if your elbows bent the other way?

Why do we call it "rush hour" when no one's going faster than 5 m.p.h.?

If all the nations in the world are in debt, where in the world did all that money go?

Why are women's magazines one half recipes and the other half diet and exercise tips?

If golf had never been invented, how would the meteorologist describe the size of hail?

As Noah's wife once said
to her husband, "I'd sure feel a lot
more relaxed if those two termites
were in a special container."

**If a dog jumps into your lap,
it is because he is fond of you;
but if a cat does the same thing,
it is because your lap is warmer.**
Alfred North Whitehead

Did you hear the one about the man
who ordered a self-help DVD called
"How to Handle Disappointment."
When the package arrived,
he opened it. It was empty.

**Lost, a boy went to a police officer
for help. "Do you think we'll ever
find my mom and dad?" the boy asked.
"It might take a little time," the officer
said. "There are so many places
they could hide."**

Retirement is when your favorite piece
of software is a pillow.

You're not a college student anymore when...

- Overturned orange crates no longer suffice in the living room.

- You know where the vacuum cleaner is and what dish detergent is for.

- 6 a.m. is when you get up, not when you're just getting into bed.

- There's no mold growing in the bottom of your coffee mug.

- Your parents aren't paying your rent or buying your books.

- A fire in the frying pan isn't a cause for hilarity.

Do not look back on happiness,
or dream of it in the future.
You are only sure of today;
do not let yourself be cheated out of it.
Henry Ward Beecher

**Time is a very precious gift of God;
so precious that it's only given
to us moment by moment.**
Amelia Barr

If it weren't for the optimist,
the pessimist wouldn't know
how happy he isn't.

**A pessimist is someone who
has a difficulty for every solution.**

An optimist is someone who can enjoy
the scenery while on a detour.

**Instead of castles in the clouds,
a pessimist builds slums in the air.**

Q&A Time

Q: Why do seagulls live near
the sea?
A: Because if they lived near
the bay, they'd be bagels!

Q: What did one escalator say
to the other?
A: I think I'm coming down with
something.

Q: Where would a cat refuse
to go?
A: To the flea market!

Q: Why did everyone make such
a fuss over the gray tabby?
A: Because she was extremely
purrrsonable.

Close Quarters

Two sardines wanted to go to a ballgame, and were discussing how to get there. "Let's take the subway to the stadium," suggested one.

"No way!" protested the other. "I don't want to get packed in like commuters!"

A chip on the shoulder
is a good indication that
there's wood higher up.

**The employee who can smile
when things go wrong is probably
on his way home for the day.**

A clear conscience is the sure
sign of a bad memory.
Mark Twain

**The beginning of wisdom
is to call things by their right names.**

Good Thought

Keep your words sweet today—you
may have to eat them tomorrow.

A bird in the hand makes blowing
your nose really difficult.

Money talks, and usually it says
"Good-bye."

A single solid fact can ruin a
perfectly good argument.

An early bird may catch the worm,
but the early worm gets eaten.

Gift Ideas

For someone who wants to go someplace really expensive, there's the local gas station.

For your sweetie who's asking for diamonds, there's a deck of cards.

For someone you want to really blow away, there's a heavy-duty fan.

For the person who expects to find something in the driveway that goes from 0 to 150 in 1 second flat, there's a shiny new bathroom scale.

In a cat's eyes,
all things belong to cats.
Proverb

**The chains of habit are generally
too small to be felt until they are
too strong to be broken.**
Samuel Johnson

Why not seize pleasure at once?
How often is happiness destroyed by
preparation, foolish preparation!
Jane Austen

**Everything is funny as long
as it is happening to somebody else.**
Will Rogers

Nostalgia Sunday

For the theme of this year's church picnic, the committee chose "A Walk Down Memory Lane." That's why one old-timer brought his horse and buggy. On the buggy, he attached a sign that said, "Energy efficient vehicle. Runs on oats and grass. Caution: Do not step in exhaust."

As soon as you sit down
to a cup of hot coffee,
the boss will ask you
to do something which
will last until the coffee is cold.

**Why do we call it
"getting away from it all"
when we have to take three suitcases
full of clothes, games for the kids,
our laptop and cell phone?**

Feel tense and irritable?
Have a headache? Then do what
it says on a bottle of aspirin: "Take two"
and "Keep away from children."

Sometimes the best
helping hand is the one that
gives a firm push.

**One of the most striking
differences between a cat
and a lie is that a cat
has only nine lives.**
Mark Twain

Heard about the two egotists
who met for lunch? It was an
I for an I the whole time.

**If God had meant for us to
touch our toes, He would have
put them closer to our fingers.**

Be bold, be bold,
and everywhere be bold.
Herbert Spenser

**An object in possession
seldom retains the same charm
that it had in pursuit.**
Pliny the Younger

If you hear that someone is
speaking ill of you, instead of
trying to defend yourself, you
should say: "He obviously does
not know me very well, since
there are so many other faults
he could have mentioned."
Epictetus

An oxymoron, without a doubt...

- Genuine imitation

- Valuable junk

- Sanitary landfill

- New classic

- Government organization

- Seriously funny

- Accurate rumor

- Clearly misunderstood statement
- Pretty ugly
- Soft rock
- Bankrupt millionaire
- Working vacation
- Dark light
- Small crowd

Rule the World

The preacher and his wife came home from the hospital with their first baby, a son. The new mother saw to his every need day in and day out while her husband spent the day in his study thinking deep thoughts about the state of the world. After several weeks, fatigue took its toll on Mom, and one day at lunch she complained to her husband.

"Remember, my dear," he pontificated, "that the hand that rocks the cradle is the hand that rules the world."

"Very true," replied his wife. "So suppose you rule the world this afternoon while I go shopping?"

None so empty,
as those who are full of themselves.
Benjamin Whichcote

A good example is the best sermon.
Benjamin Franklin

None are more apt to praise others
extravagantly than those who desire
to be praised themselves.

It is foolish to tear one's hair in
grief, as though sorrow would be
made less by baldness.
Cicero

The test of good manners is the
ability to put up with bad ones.

**Some of us think holding
on makes us strong;
but sometimes it is letting go.**
Hermann Hesse

Mishaps are like knives that either
serve us or cut us, as we grasp them
by the blade or the handle.
James Russell Lowell

Success comes before work
only in the dictionary.

**Could we change our attitude,
we should not only see life differently,
but life itself would come to be
different. Life would undergo a
change of appearance because
we ourselves had undergone a
change in attitude.**
Katherine Mansfield

I am not afraid of storms,
for I am learning how to sail my ship.
Louisa May Alcott

Adam and Eve

After the Fall, Adam covered himself with a fig leaf. Eve covered herself, too, with a fig leaf. Then she looked at the fig leaf, gazed at all the trees in the Garden, and decided to try on a sycamore leaf, a birch leaf, a maple leaf, an oak leaf...

Help!

A man in obvious distress went up to the pharmacy counter and said, "Please! Can you give me something for my head?"

"Why?" the pharmacist replied. "What would I do with it?"

Nine requisites for contented living:
Health enough to make work a pleasure.
Wealth enough to support your needs.
Strength to battle with difficulties
and overcome them.
Grace enough to confess your sins
and forsake them.
Patience enough to toil until some good
is accomplished.

Charity enough to see some good
in your neighbor.
Love enough to move you to be useful
and helpful to others.
Faith enough to make real
the things of God.
Hope enough to remove all anxious fears
concerning the future.

Johann von Goethe

Sunday School

A Sunday school teacher was telling her class about Lot and his family's escape from the town of Sodom. "Lot was warned to take his wife and flee out of the city, but his wife looked back and turned into a pillar of salt."

A little girl sitting in the back of the room raised her hand. "Miss Jones, then what happened to the flea?"

To succeed in the world,
it is much more necessary to possess
the penetration to discover
who is a fool than to discover
who is a clever man.
Cato the Elder

**Alas, after a certain age, every man
is responsible for his face.**
Albert Camus

If you want a place in the sun,
you've got to expect a few blisters.

He Said, She Said

She: You said you live off the spat of the land. Don't you mean the fat of the land?
He: No. I'm a marriage counselor.

He: Honey, I bought you an A.M. radio.
She: Oh, sweetheart, I really wanted one I could listen to at night.

She: You look like my first husband.
He: Really? So how many times have you been married?
She: None.

He: Aren't you ready yet?
She: Next time we go out, let's change jobs. You get the kids bathed and in their PJs, fix their snacks, leave contact information for the sitter, and I'll pace the living room floor and look at my watch every five minutes.

He: Uh-oh, I just ran that red light.
She: Don't worry, dear. The trooper behind you did the same thing.

He: If you give me your phone number, I'll give you a call.
She: It's in the book.
He: Awesome! What's your name?
She: That's in the book, too.

If you want to see your long-lost relatives, simply buy a beachfront vacation home.

Let a smile be your umbrella, and you'll get a mouthful of rain.

If everyone obeyed the Ten Commandments, what would the 24-hour news channels talk about?

They say that kids today don't know the value of a dollar. Why, they certainly do! That's why they always ask for fifty.

I must say I hate money, but it's the
lack of it that I hate most.
Katherine Mansfield

**You cannot do a kindness too soon,
for you never know how soon
it will be too late.**
Ralph Waldo Emerson

If you ask God to move a mountain,
don't be surprised when
He hands you a shovel.

**There are times in everyone's life
when something constructive is born
out of adversity—when things seem so
bad that you've got to grab your fate
by the shoulders and shake it.**

High, High C

There was a young girl in the choir
Whose voice went up higher and higher,
Till one Sunday night
It vanished from sight,
And turned up the next day in the spire.

If you have a garden and a library,
you have everything you need.
Cicero

Enough is as good as a feast.
Proverb

May you have warm words on a cool
evening, a full moon on a dark night,
and a smooth road all the way
to your door.
Irish Toast

There is not a more pleasing exercise
of the mind than gratitude.
Joseph Addison

A smile costs nothing but gives much. It enriches those who receive without making poorer those who give. It takes but a moment, but the memory of it sometimes lasts forever. None is so rich or mighty that he cannot get along without it, and none is so poor that he cannot be made rich by it. Yet a smile cannot be bought, begged, borrowed, or stolen, for it is something that is of no value to anyone until it is given away. Some people are too tired to give you a smile. Give them one of yours, as none needs a smile so much as he who has no more to give.

Three Wishes

Three men were stranded on a tiny, isolated island. One day a lamp washed up on the beach, and one of the men rubbed it. Out popped a genie. "I can grant three wishes," said the genie, "and since there are three of you, each of you will get one wish."

"I'm tired of being on this island," said the first man, "and I wish to go home." The man disappeared in an instant.

"And you?" said the genie to the second man.

"I feel the same way," said the man, "and there's nothing I want more than to go home." Poof! He was gone. The genie's gaze fell on the third man.

"I'm lonely here, sitting all by myself!" he said, "and I wish my friends would come back!"

Daffy Definitions

Subdivision: A place where they chop down trees and then name the streets after them.

Slowest lane of traffic: The one you're in.

Creative writing: Style most often found on tax forms.

Parking valet: Demolition derby wanna-be.

Vision: What people credit you with when you guess right.

University: An academic institution with a stadium seating more than 75 thousand.

Ouch!: The voice of experience.

Garage: Building with a house attached.

Middle age: When you start dimming the lights for economic, not romantic, reasons.

Acorn: An oak in a nutshell.

The best advice you can give people is find out what they're going to do anyway, and then advise them to do it.

Did you hear the one about the girl who applied to an on-line dating service? She said she liked water sports and formal dress, and they matched her up with a penguin.

Says the baby snake, "Mom, are we poisonous?" "We certainly are," Mom replies. "Oh no," says baby snake, "because I just bit my tongue!"

Driving Rain

A storm broke loose, and a sheet of rain streamed down the windshield, making vision almost impossible. In fact, the car almost collided with another. The passenger said, "Don't you think we ought to pull off the road until the rain tapers off and we can see better?"

"Nah," answered the driver. "It won't make any difference, because I left my glasses at home on the kitchen table."

People seldom improve when
they have no other model but
themselves to copy.
Oliver Goldsmith

**If you board the wrong train,
it is no use running along the
corridor in the other direction.**
Dietrich Bonhoeffer

No matter how much the cats
fight, there always seems to be
plenty of kittens.
Abraham Lincoln

A gentle word, a kind look,
a good-natured smile can work
wonders and accomplish miracles.
William Hazlitt

Without ambition one starts
nothing. Without work one
finishes nothing. The prize will
not be sent to you. You have to
win it. The man who knows how
will always have a job. The man
who also knows why will always
be his boss. As to methods there
may be a million and then some,
but principles are few. The man
who grasps principles can suc-
cessfully select his own methods.
The man who tries methods,
ignoring principles,
is sure to have trouble.
Ralph Waldo Emerson

Competitive Edge

The only two barbershops on Main Street were in fierce competition with each other. One put a sign in his window advertising haircuts for $7. Not to be outdone, his competitor displayed a sign that read: "We repair $7 haircuts."

A wise person turns great
troubles into little ones and little
ones into none at all.
Proverb

**So much has been said and sung
of beautiful young girls, why
doesn't somebody wake up to
the beauty of old women?**
Harriet Beecher Stowe

Best be yourself,
imperial, plain and true!
Robert Browning

So Punny

The nuclear physicist was exhausted at the end of the week. Turns out he had too many ions in the fire.

Two geology students were dating, but then she broke it off. "He kept taking me for granite," she said.

She had a photographic memory, but it obviously wasn't developed yet.

The cross-eyed teacher decided to pursue another career. Turns out she couldn't control her pupils.

Never ever iron a four-leaf clover. You'd only be pressing your luck.

Mama cat gave birth in the city park and was cited for littering.

The farmer's wife complained about the ducks that swam in the pond outside. They kept waking her up at the quack of dawn.

The barista in the corner shop quit after she got tired of the daily grind.

The athlete had a fear of hurdles, but then he got over it.

"Look into my eyes.
You want your freedom.
You want to jump."

Keeping Up Appearances

An ambitious entrepreneur set up a well-appointed office for himself. On his first day behind his executive-level desk, a man entered the reception area. Hoping to impress a potential client, the entrepreneur picked up his desk telephone and pretended he was in the middle of a high-volume deal with a major client. Finally, he hung up and greeted his visitor. "May I help you?" he asked.

"Sure," the visitor replied. "I've come to hook up your phone!"

Do not worry; eat three square meals a day; say your prayers; be courteous to your creditors; keep your digestion good; exercise; go slow and easy. Maybe there are other things your special case requires to make you happy; but, my friend, these I reckon will give you a good lift.

Abraham Lincoln

Q&A Time

Q: Why was the kitten afraid
of the tree?
A: Because of its bark.

Q: What did one math book say
to the other?
A: Boy, have we got problems!

Q: How do you catch a unique cat?
A: Unique up on it.

Q: Why can't two elephants go
swimming at the same time?
A: Because they've only got one
pair of trunks between them.

Those who begin too much
accomplish little.
Proverb

**Short as life is,
we make it still shorter by the
careless waste of time.**
Victor Hugo

Put all your eggs in one basket—
and watch that basket.
Mark Twain

Without risk,
faith is an impossibility.
Søren Kierkegaard

**Happiness is not a horse;
you cannot harness it.**
Proverb

Perhaps the most delightful
friendships are those in which
there is much agreement,
much disputation, and yet
more personal liking.
George Eliot

Heard about...

- The man who got right back on his bike every time he fell off?
  He was a firm believer in recycling.

- The couple who ate dinner at the German restaurant? They didn't care for the sauerkraut, but the wurst was yet to come.

- The shoe store with a "Buy one, get one free" offer? But aren't all shoes sold that way?

- The skunk that was a faithful churchgoer? He had his own pew.

- The expensive restaurant serving steaks "good to the last bite"? Unfortunately, the last bite was also the first.

- The latest food craze from Britain, the BBC diet? It stands for Buy Bigger Clothes.

- The kid in the spelling bee who was asked to spell Mississippi? "Which one," he asked, "the river or the state?"

- The chicken who would go only half way across the road? She wanted to lay it on the line.

**"Ah yes!
Yesterday's entrée was fish."**

The habit of being
uniformly considerate toward
others will bring increased
happiness to you.
Grenville Kleiser

**When we begin to take our
failures non-seriously,
it means we are ceasing to be
afraid of them. It is of immense
importance to learn
to laugh at ourselves.**
Katherine Mansfield

The best place to find
a helping hand is at the end of
your own arm.
Proverb

This is the beginning of a new day. God has given me this day to use as I will. I can waste it or use it for good, but what I do today is important, because I am exchanging a day of my life for it! When tomorrow comes, this day will be gone forever, leaving in its place something that I have traded for it. I want it to be gain, and not loss; good, and not evil; success, and not failure; in order that I shall not regret the price I have paid for it.

Before we set our hearts too
much upon anything, let us
examine how happy they are
who already possess it.
François de La Rochefoucauld

**When confronted with two
courses of action, I jot down
on a piece of paper all the
arguments in favor of each one,
then on the opposite side I write
the arguments against each one.
Then by weighing the arguments
pro and con and cancelling them
out, one against the other,
I take the course indicated
by what remains.**
Benjamin Franklin

It is common to overlook what is
near by keeping the eye fixed on
something remote.
Samuel Johnson

True Love

A handsome tomcat was courting a pretty Persian, and under the light of the moon, he cooed in her ear, "Darling, I'd die for you." She looked up into his eyes and asked, "How many times?"

History Repeated

The tour guide, pointing to a building, said that it had been there for 300 years. "Nothing has changed," he told the crowd, "not even a stone has been moved or replaced."

A voice came from the back: "Must've been the same landlord I've got."

Some people are easily
entertained. All you have to do is
sit down and listen to them.

**The easiest person to
deceive is one's own self.**
Edward G Bulwer-Lytton

There is nothing like staying at
home for real comfort.
Jane Austen

**The sting of criticism is the
truth in it.**

No one can make you feel
inferior without your consent.
Eleanor Roosevelt

**While there's life,
there's hope.**
Cicero

Prayer requires more of the
heart than of the tongue.
Adam Clarke

The cat is the animal to whom
the Creator gave the biggest
eye, the softest fur, the most
supremely delicate nostrils,
a mobile ear, an unrivaled paw
and a curved claw borrowed
from the rose-tree.
Colette

**It's easier to know how to do
than it is to do.**
Proverb

Have you heard about the boy
computer mouse that met a girl
computer mouse?
They clicked immediately.

He could be rich and famous,
but two things are holding him
back—he's broke and nobody
knows him.

Dogs aren't as smart as some
people think. I took mine to
obedience school and I learned
to sit, heel and fetch three
weeks before he did.

New Owner

Along the hiking trail, there was a small diner. One hiker, needing a little refreshment, stopped in and sat down. An elk came over to his table and handed him a menu. The hiker stared in astonishment.

"What's the matter?" asked the elk. "Haven't you seen an elk with a menu before?"

"It's not that," said the hiker. "I'm just surprised that the bear finally sold this place."

The worst part about spending $300 on an evening out without the kids is getting home and suspecting that the sitter had a better time than you did.

The freshman was puzzled why her professor needed three pairs of glasses. "I have one pair for reading," he explained, "and one pair for distance. The third pair I use when I need to look for the other two."

Two boll weevils grew up in the South. One went to Hollywood and became a famous movie star, but the other stayed home and never did very much at all. Needless to say, this one was known as the lesser of two weevils.

"At heart, I'm a jungle cat stalking my prey."

Sleep.
Stretch.
Snooze.
Repeat.